LET'S FIND OUT! THE HUMAN BODY

THE MUSCLES IN YOUR BODY

BOBI MARTIN

Britannica
Educational Publishing

IN ASSOCIATION WITH

ROSEN
EDUCATIONAL SERVICES

Published in 2015 by Britannica Educational Publishing (a trademark of Encyclopædia Britannica, Inc.) in association with The Rosen Publishing Group, Inc.
29 East 21st Street, New York, NY 10010

Distributed exclusively by Rosen Publishing.
To see additional Britannica Educational Publishing titles, go to rosenpublishing.com.

First Edition

<u>Britannica Educational Publishing</u>
J.E. Luebering: Director, Core Reference Group
Mary Rose McCudden: Editor, Britannica Student Encyclopedia

<u>Rosen Publishing</u>
Hope Lourie Killcoyne: Executive Editor
Shalini Saxena: Editor
Nelson Sá: Art Director
Michael Moy: Designer
Cindy Reiman: Photography Manager

Library of Congress Cataloging-in-Publication Data

Martin, Bobi, author.
The muscles in your body/Bobi Martin. — First edition.
       pages cm. — (Let's find out! The human body)
Includes bibliographical references and index.
ISBN 978-1-62275-651-3 (library bound) — ISBN 978-1-62275-652-0 (pbk.) — ISBN 978-1-62275-653-7 (6-pack)
1. Muscles — Juvenile literature. 2. Musculoskeletal system — Juvenile literature. 3. Human anatomy — Juvenile literature. I. Title.
QM151.M37 2015
611.73 — dc23
                                                                                          2014012810

Manufactured in the United States of America

Photo credits: Cover © iStockphoto.com/pailoolom; p. 1, interior pages Lightspring/Shutterstock.com; pp. 4, 21 Blend Images/Shutterstock.com; p. 5 Emine Bayram/iStock/Thinkstock; pp. 6, 7, 8, 10, 12, 27 Encyclopædia Britannica, Inc.; p. 9 Jupiterimages/BananaStock/Thinkstock; p. 11 © iStockphoto.com/Juanmonino; p. 13 Manfred Kage/Science Source; p. 14 Spike Walker/The Image Bank/Getty Images; p. 15 ejwhite/Shutterstock.com; p. 16 BlueRingMedia/Shutterstock.com; p. 17 monkeybusinessimages/iStock/Thinkstock: p. 18 Rob Marmion/Shutterstock.com; p. 19 © iStockphoto.com/isitsharp; p. 20 Jacek Chabraszewski/Shutterstock.com; p. 22 Daniel H. Bailey/Photolibrary/Getty Images; p. 23 shutterbugger/iStock/Thinkstock; p. 24 Image Point Fr/Shutterstock.com; p. 25 jstudio/Shutterstock.com; p. 26 Creatas Images/Thinkstock; p. 28 TsuneoMP/Shutterstock.com; p. 29 © iStockphoto.com/Martenot.

CONTENTS

MUSCLES WORK AROUND THE CLOCK

Muscles are an important part of your body. Anything you can imagine yourself doing uses muscles. You need muscles to run, throw a ball, or ride a bike. You also use muscles at times when it seems like you are not doing anything. It takes muscles to smile, read a book, or swallow food.

Even when you are sleeping, many of your muscles

Throwing and catching a ball is a good way to work the muscles in your hands, arms, and shoulders.

are still hard at work. Muscles in your digestive system are turning the food you ate for dinner into fuel for your body. The muscle in your heart

THINK ABOUT IT
Why don't all of your muscles sleep when you do? Why is this important?

is beating and pumping blood. Muscles in your chest are helping you breathe. Your muscles work all day and all night, too.

When people are asleep, they breathe more slowly, but many of their muscles are still working hard.

TYPES OF MUSCLES

Your body has three types of muscles: skeletal muscle, cardiac muscle, and smooth muscle.

Skeletal muscle connects to your bones. These muscles come in all shapes and sizes because they do different jobs. A muscle in your ears is your smallest muscle. It moves the smallest bone you have. Muscles in your

Humans have over 700 muscles, but grasshoppers have 900. If people could jump like grasshoppers, they could leap across a football field in one bound!

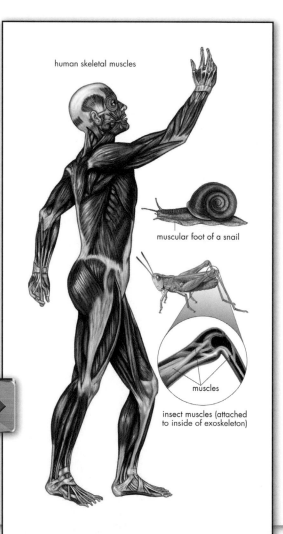

human skeletal muscles

muscular foot of a snail

muscles

insect muscles (attached to inside of exoskeleton)

COMPARE AND CONTRAST
How are the muscles in your ears and legs the same?
How are they different?

cardiac muscle cells

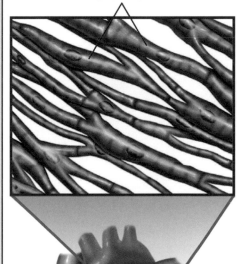

heart

legs are large and strong. They must move and support your whole body.

Cardiac muscle is located in the heart. It pumps blood by squeezing and relaxing in a regular pattern of beats called the heartbeat.

Smooth muscle lines the intestines, stomach, and other organs in the body. These muscles are not connected to bones. They control what your organs do without you having to think about it.

The heart is a network of highly branched cardiac cells. The cells are organized into layers of tissue that are wrapped around the chambers of the heart.

INVOLUNTARY AND VOLUNTARY MUSCLES

Your cardiac muscle and your smooth muscles are also called involuntary muscles. That means you cannot control them even if you try! These muscles work without you having to think about them. Most of your involuntary muscles, such as the

The smooth muscles in your stomach contract and relax to help move food from your stomach to your intestines.

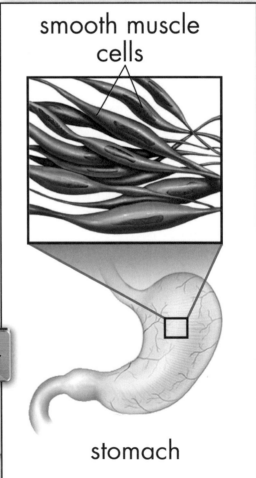

smooth muscle cells

stomach

THINK ABOUT IT

Why do we need involuntary muscles? Why is it important that skeletal muscles are voluntary muscles?

smooth muscles in your lungs, stomach, and blood vessels, are controlled by your nervous system. The nervous system is a network of nerves that send messages between the brain and other parts of the body. The cardiac muscle controls itself, but it can also respond to messages from the nervous system.

Because you choose when you want your skeletal muscles to move, they are called voluntary muscles. When you turn a page of a book, you are using voluntary muscles. You think about turning the page and then your arm, hand, and fingers work together to make that happen.

Reading uses more muscles than you might think. You need the voluntary muscles in your eyes, neck, shoulders, arms, hands, and fingers as well as many involuntary muscles.

SKELETAL MUSCLES

Strong cordlike tissues called tendons connect your skeletal muscles to your bones. Skeletal muscles move your bones by **contracting** and relaxing. Muscles can only pull your bones; they cannot push, so they often work in pairs. First, one muscle contracts and

When you bend your arm, your biceps muscle contracts and the triceps relaxes. To stretch your arm flat, the triceps contracts and the biceps relaxes.

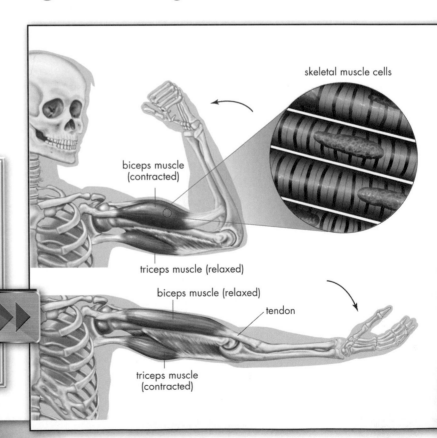

skeletal muscle cells

biceps muscle (contracted)

triceps muscle (relaxed)

biceps muscle (relaxed)

tendon

triceps muscle (contracted)

Contracting means tightening up and getting shorter.

pulls the bone one way. Then that muscle relaxes, and the second muscle contracts to pull the bone back again.

Besides moving your bones, your skeletal muscles have other important jobs. They help hold your posture (the position of the body). They also help keep your body at the right temperature. When muscles contract and relax, they make heat that warms your body. When you are cold, your muscles may shiver, which means your muscles contract and relax very quickly many times. That process makes heat to warm you up again.

 Although your muscles help keep your body warm, you still need to wear a coat on cold days.

To tell a muscle to move, your brain sends a message along a type of nerve called a motor nerve. Motor nerves end in the fibers of your muscles. These nerves release chemicals into the muscle. This process starts a wave of activity that creates the energy that moves your muscle. Skeletal muscles perform difficult tasks quickly. They sometimes get tired and need to rest.

Skeletal muscles are made up of bundles

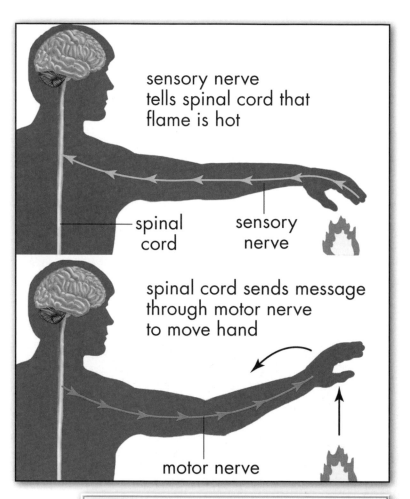

sensory nerve tells spinal cord that flame is hot

spinal cord

sensory nerve

spinal cord sends message through motor nerve to move hand

motor nerve

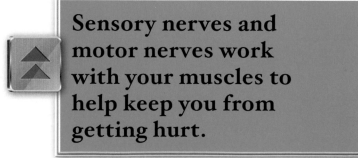

Sensory nerves and motor nerves work with your muscles to help keep you from getting hurt.

of long, thin fibers. If you look at skeletal muscle under a microscope, it looks striped. This is because the ends of some fibers lay over the ends of other fibers. The parts that overlap each other look like dark stripes.

THINK ABOUT IT

Why do the overlapping fibers look darker than the other fibers?

The dark area where the ends of skeletal muscle fibers overlap is called a Z line.

SMOOTH MUSCLES

Not all muscles look striped. Some muscles look smooth under a microscope. Smooth muscles work in the hollow parts of your body. The smooth muscles in your lungs help you breathe. Smooth muscles also move food through your stomach and intestines. Smooth muscles contract in all directions. They use less energy than skeletal muscles because they contract and relax more slowly.

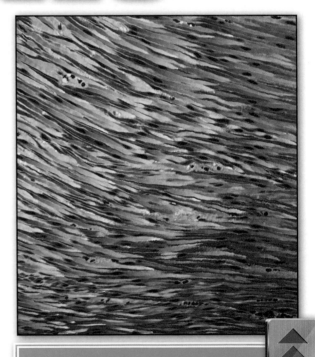

Smooth muscles are made of layers of fibers. Each layer runs in a different direction. This is why smooth muscles can contract in all directions.

COMPARE AND CONTRAST

Both smooth muscles and skeletal muscles contract. Why do skeletal muscles tire more quickly than smooth muscles?

Your nervous system controls your smooth muscles for you. Imagine if you had to think about each breath you took or if you had to tell your stomach to digest your food. You would be too busy thinking about those basic activities to be able to do anything else!

The skeletal muscles in your tongue and mouth help you chew and swallow your food. Smooth muscles in your stomach and intestines help you digest your food.

CARDIAC MUSCLE

Cardiac muscle is found only in your heart. Like your skeletal muscles, cardiac muscle looks striped. The fibers of cardiac muscle form the four hollow areas of your heart, which are called chambers. When cardiac muscle contracts and relaxes, blood is pumped in and out of the chambers. Blood coming from your heart carries oxygen to your

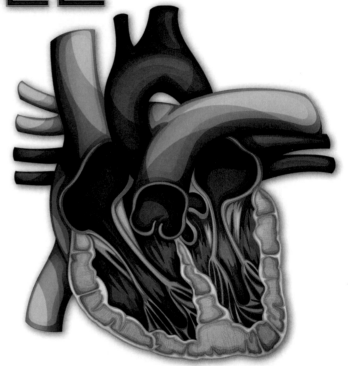

Cardiac muscle beats about 60 to 70 times per minute. More than 4 quarts (3.8 liters) of blood pass through the heart every minute.

> **A rhythm is a regular pattern of beats.**

muscles and to other parts of your body.

Cardiac muscle is involuntary. A special strip of cardiac muscle releases bursts of electricity that keep your heart beating in a regular rhythm. That rhythm is your heartbeat. Cardiac muscle contracts about 60 to 70 times a minute. When you are excited or get startled, the nervous system tells the heart to beat faster. Cardiac muscle rests between each contraction, so it never gets tired.

> **A special tool called a stethoscope allows doctors to listen to the rhythm of your heartbeat.**

EXERCISE THOSE MUSCLES

Muscles are made to move! Being active for an hour or more every day helps keep your muscles healthy. Muscles need three types of exercise to be at their best. Aerobic exercise makes you breathe faster and gets your heart pumping. Strength exercises help your muscles get stronger. And exercise

Doing strength exercises like push-ups is important to help muscles get strong and stay strong.

COMPARE AND CONTRAST

In what ways are skateboarding, basketball, and gymnastics good exercise? How are they different?

that helps you stretch your muscles helps keep them flexible.

Skateboarding, dancing, and gymnastics are some fun aerobic activities. Sports that make you run or move fast, like basketball, soccer, or hockey, are good aerobic exercise, too. Aerobics are good for your cardiac muscle. Exercising your heart this way keeps it strong. It also helps your heart pump more oxygen through your body.

Playing a sport like soccer is a fun way to make sure your muscles get the aerobic exercise they need.

19

Some exercises, like riding a bike, are good for both your skeletal muscles and your cardiac muscle.

Activity that makes your skeletal muscles work hard helps make them stronger. That gives them more power and helps them work longer before getting tired. Push-ups, riding your bike, and swinging across the monkey bars make your muscles stronger. Playing baseball and tennis strengthens muscles, too.

Stretching keeps your skeletal muscles flexible so you can bend and reach better. Touching your toes or stretching your arms toward the ceiling are simple stretches you can do almost anywhere. Martial

THINK ABOUT IT

Some activities help your cardiac and skeletal muscles get stronger. Some activities keep you flexible. Why are all of these activities important to your body?

arts, dancing, tumbling, and gymnastics are fun activities that help you stretch your muscles and stay flexible. Whatever type of exercise you choose, being active keeps your muscles healthy.

When something is flexible, it is able to move or bend in more than one direction.

MUSCLES AND SPORTS

Doing the same action over and over helps your muscles remember it. This is called muscle memory. For example, when you practice dribbling a ball or doing a backflip, muscle memory helps your muscles do the action better and faster.

Practicing an activity may not make you perfect, but it will help you do it better and faster.

Smart athletes warm up their muscles before they exercise so they can perform better. Warming up also helps prevent injury to muscles.

Muscles that have been resting for a long time are cold and do not work as well as they could. Before playing a sport, it is important to warm up your muscles with a few minutes of light exercise, like jumping jacks or jogging. When your muscles are warmed up, they can take in more oxygen. This helps them contract with more power so you can run faster or jump higher.

THINK ABOUT IT
Why do some people practice a sport or an activity every day?

MUSCLE INJURIES

Muscles can be injured if they are used too hard or for too long at one time. Skeletal muscles get tired more quickly than other muscles. They need time to rest. An overworked muscle might contract too hard and not be able to relax. This can cause a painful cramp. Gently rubbing the sore area usually helps the muscle relax again.

Some muscle injuries are very painful and may need special treatment to get better.

COMPARE AND CONTRAST

In what ways are muscle cramps and muscle strains similar? How are the ways you take care of them different?

When a muscle is stretched too far, it is called a pulled muscle or a muscle strain. This kind of injury can cause the area around the muscle to bruise or get swollen. Resting your muscles when they feel weak or tired will help prevent injury.

A muscle cramp usually goes away quickly. Gently rubbing or massaging the area often helps.

THE MUSCLES IN YOUR FACE

When you think about the muscles in your body, you probably don't think about your face. But it is full of muscles! Most facial muscles do not pull on your bones. Instead, they pull on your skin. Whether you are happy, sad, angry, or surprised, your facial muscles help you show your feelings.

When you take a bite of food, you use the muscles in your jaws, lips, tongue, and cheeks. The muscles in your lips help keep food inside your

Facial muscles help us make the expressions that show how we feel. You wouldn't be able to smile or frown without the muscles in your face.

mouth. Your jaws help your teeth grind up your food. And your tongue helps move food from your mouth to your throat.

Your head and neck are full of muscles. It takes six muscles just to hold an eyeball in place and move it around.

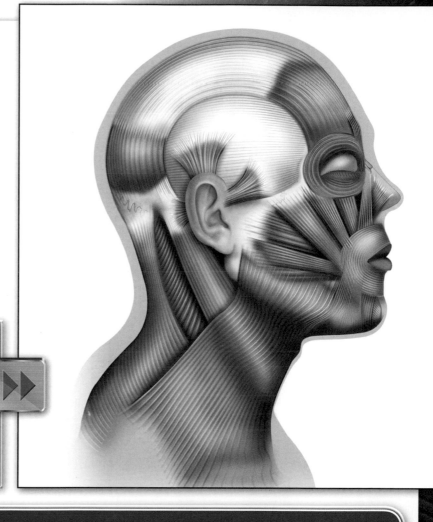

Think About It

Muscles in your lips and tongue also help you speak clearly. Try to talk without moving your lips or your tongue. Can your friends understand you?

WHAT WOULD WE DO WITHOUT MUSCLES?

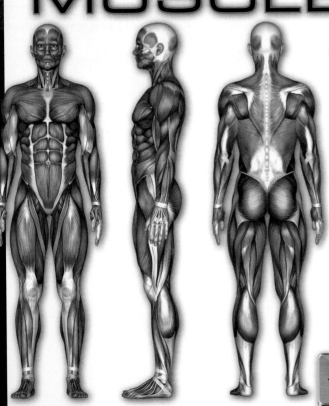

Think about all the things your muscles do for you. You use muscles to open your eyes in the morning. You use muscles to get out of bed. Your cardiac muscle keeps blood

Your body has many muscle groups that work together to help you through your day.

THINK ABOUT IT

How do your muscles help your body? In what ways can you help your muscles?

moving through your body, and your smooth muscles help your organs do their jobs. Without muscles, you would not even be able to talk or eat. Your body could not live without muscles.

Eating a variety of healthy foods and getting enough exercise every day will help keep your muscles strong and healthy. When you take good care of your muscles, they will take good care of you, too!

All girls and boys should be physically active at least an hour or more every day to build strong, healthy muscles.

GLOSSARY

aerobic Related to, or using, oxygen.

cardiac muscle The muscle in the heart.

connected Hooked together.

digestive system The parts of the body that work together to turn food into energy.

fiber A thin, threadlike strand that is part of skeletal muscle.

fuel Something that provides power or energy.

intestines Long, winding tubes in the body that help digest food.

involuntary Not done by choice.

nervous system A system of nerves that carries messages between the brain and the body.

organ Body part with a specific job, like the stomach or heart.

overlap To cover part of something.

relax To let go or get longer.

skeletal muscle Muscle that moves bones.

smooth muscle Muscle in the hollow parts of the body, like the stomach.

strain To pull or stretch with too much force.

support To hold up.

tendons Strong tissue that connects muscles to bones.

voluntary Done by choice.

FOR MORE INFORMATION

Books

Barraclough, Sue. *The Skeletal and Muscular Systems: How Can I Stand on My Head?* Chicago, IL: Heinemann Library, 2008.

Bingham, Caroline. *The Little Brainwaves Investigate...Human Body.* New York, NY: DK Publishing, 2010.

Manolis, Kay. *The Muscular System.* Minneapolis, MN: Bellwether Media, 2009.

Walker, Richard. *Eyewitness Human Body.* New York, NY: DK Publishing, 2009.

Walker, Richard, John Woodward, et al. *Human Body: A Visual Encyclopedia.* New York, NY: DK Publishing, 2012.

Websites

Because of the changing nature of Internet links, Rosen Publishing has developed an online list of websites related to the subject of this book. This site is updated regularly. Please use this link to access the list:

http://www.rosenlinks.com/LFO/Musc

INDEX